MONSTER HUNTERS

FINDING ZOMBIES

By Therese Shea

Gareth Stevens
PUBLISHING

Please visit our website, www.garethstevens.com. For a free color catalog of all our high-quality books, call toll free 1-800-542-2595 or fax 1-877-542-2596.

Library of Congress Cataloging-in-Publication Data
Names: Shea, Therese, author.
Title: Finding zombies / Therese Shea.
Description: New York : Gareth Stevens Publishing, [2026] | Series: Monster hunters | Includes index.
Identifiers: LCCN 2025001084 (print) | LCCN 2025001085 (ebook) | ISBN 9781482472233 (lib. bdg.) | ISBN 9781482472226 (paperback) | ISBN 9781482472240 (ebook)
Subjects: LCSH: Zombies–Juvenile literature.
Classification: LCC GR581 .S54 2026 (print) | LCC GR581 (ebook) | DDC 398.21–dc23/eng/20250325
LC record available at https://lccn.loc.gov/2025001084
LC ebook record available at https://lccn.loc.gov/2025001085

Published in 2026 by
Gareth Stevens Publishing
2544 Clinton Street
Buffalo, NY 14224

Copyright © 2026 Gareth Stevens Publishing

Designer: Andrea Davison-Bartolotta
Editor: Therese Shea

Photo credits: Cover, p. 1 Shutterstock AI/Shutterstock.com; cover, p. 1, series art (glowing compass rose) LoveDesignShop/Shutterstock.com; series art (cardinal compass rose) Angela Ksen/Shutterstock.com; series art (ordinal compass rose) jame05/Shutterstock.com; series art (fact box rope border) LanaN/Shutterstock.com; series art (fact box wood) EE SPACE/Shutterstock.com; series art (map background) Olha Andreichyn/Shutterstock.com; series art (curled paper background) MIGUEL G. SAAVEDRA/Shutterstock.com; series art (flat paper) Paladin12/Shutterstock.com; p. 5 (green paint) Sensvector/Shutterstock.com; p. 5 (main) leolintang/Shutterstock.com; p. 7 (right map) Sidhe/Shutterstock.com; p. 7 (left map) alvindom/Shutterstock.com; p. 7 (bottom) Romolo Tavani/Shutterstock.com; p. 8 Raggedstone/Shutterstock.com; pp. 9, 11, 13, 15,17, 18, 23 (all maps) Peter Hermes Furian/Shutterstock.com; p. 9 (background) Helen Hotson/Shutterstock.com; p. 11 (background) Zacarias da Mata/Shutterstock.com; p. 13 (top) Kim Diaz Holm/ File:Giant draugr by Kim Diaz Holm (cropped).jpg/Wikimedia Commons; p. 15 (bottom) Dick Thomas Johnson/Flickr.com; p. 17 (bottom) Everett Collection/Shutterstock.com; p. 19 Jean-noel Lafargue/File:Zombie haiti ill artlibre jnl.png/Wikimedia Commons; p. 21 (inset) Kiattipong/Shutterstock.com; p. 21 (main) Sergey Shubin/Shutterstock.com; p. 23 (poster) BFA/Alamy Stock Photo; p. 23 (bottom) File:EvansCityCemetery PA.jpg/Wikimedia Commons; p. 25 Miroslav Halama/Shutterstock.com; p. 27 (map) Rainer Lesniewski/Shutterstock.com; p. 27 (main) Alan Budman/Shutterstock.com; pp. 28, 29 (map) Janos Levente/Shutterstock.com; pp. 28, 29 (paper) AKaiser/Shutterstock.com.

All rights reserved. No part of this book may be reproduced in any form without permission in writing from the publisher, except by a reviewer.

Printed in the United States of America

CPSIA compliance information: Batch #CSGS26: For further information contact Gareth Stevens at 1-800-542-2595.

CONTENTS

Hungry Zombies! 4
First Stop, Greece 6
Revenants 8
Grave Discoveries 10
The Draugr 12
The Jiangshi 14
Next Stop, Haiti 16
Zombies Go Hollywood 20
Zombie Reality? 24
Zombie Culture 26
Zombies on the Map 28
Glossary 30
For More Information 31
Index 32

Words in the glossary appear in **bold** type the first time they are used in the text.

HUNGRY ZOMBIES!

Imagine you're at the park with some friends. Suddenly, you see a group of kids walking toward you. They're actually shuffling their feet more than walking. They don't look so well. Their clothes are ripped. Their skin is kind of gray. They're groaning a lot too. Whoa—that one's missing an arm and that one's missing an eyeball. Don't invite them to play soccer with you. They're zombies!

Let's track zombie **myths** around the world. Not all zombies are brains-hungry creatures—they're all bad news, though!

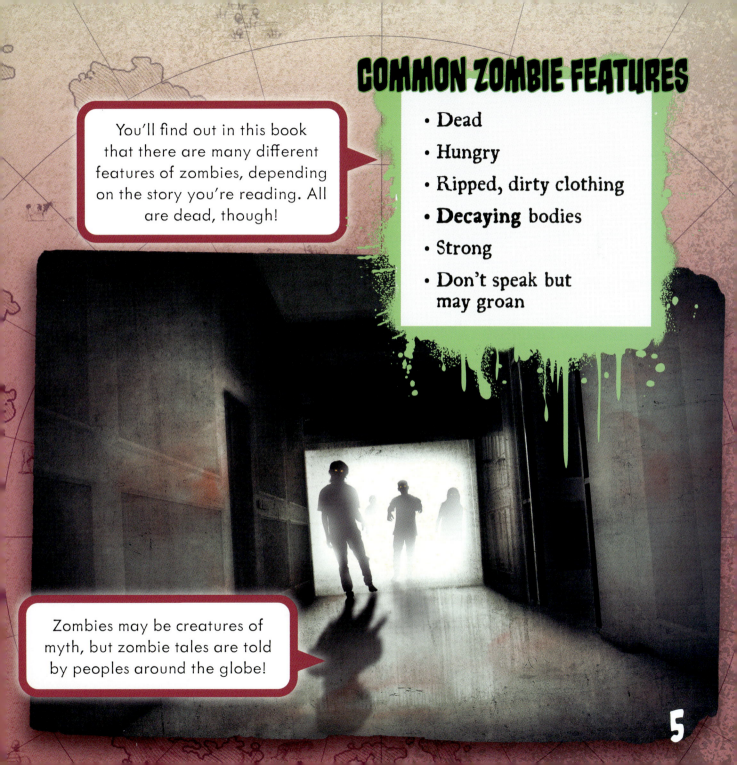

COMMON ZOMBIE FEATURES

- Dead
- Hungry
- Ripped, dirty clothing
- **Decaying** bodies
- Strong
- Don't speak but may groan

You'll find out in this book that there are many different features of zombies, depending on the story you're reading. All are dead, though!

Zombies may be creatures of myth, but zombie tales are told by peoples around the globe!

First Stop, Greece

You'll need to look at some maps to get around as you collect tales about zombies. Some people think the ancient Greeks believed in zombies. Head to the country of Greece to learn more.

Archaeologists in Greece have found several graves from more than 2,000 years ago that may show at least a belief in zombies. Skeletons in these graves have rocks or other heavy things on top of them. Many think this strange custom must have been done to stop the dead bodies from rising again!

MODERN GREECE

ANCIENT GREECE

Ancient Greece was larger than the country of Greece today. Compare the borders in the two maps.

Behind the Myth

Ancient Greek writers talked about people rising from the dead and taking **revenge** on enemies. It was a common belief that the dead didn't have to stay dead.

Sometimes zombies are called "the undead."

REVENANTS

Like zombies in stories, a revenant is a being—or a body—that has returned from the dead. Archaeologists have found evidence, or proof, of a belief in revenants in graves in many places in Europe.

To head to another graveyard to see this for yourself, you'll travel from Greece to England in northeastern Europe. The compass rose on the map will help. This is the circular tool that shows the directions on the map.

The four main directions, called the cardinal directions, are north (N), south (S), east (E), and west (W). The ordinal directions are between the cardinal directions. They are northeast (NE), southeast (SE), northwest (NW), and southwest (SW).

GRAVE DISCOVERIES

In some graves in England from around 300 CE, bodies were buried facedown. This was unusual as most bodies are buried faceup. Perhaps this was a way to make it harder for these bodies to rise and become the undead? It's hard for archaeologists to know for sure, but it's a possibility.

Graves in nearby Ireland from a few centuries later contain skeletons with stones in their mouths. That might have been done to prevent the undead from biting if they rose again!

Behind the Myth

Because of their proximity, or nearness, the people of Ireland and the United Kingdom (UK) share some common myths. A belief in revenants—zombies—may have been one such myth.

The United Kingdom is made up of the countries of England, Scotland, Wales, and Northern Ireland. The Republic of Ireland is a separate country.

11

THE DRAUGR

From Ireland and the UK, it won't be too far to travel to the Nordic countries of Europe: Denmark, Finland, Iceland, Norway, and Sweden. This is where Norse myths come from—and the zombie-like monster called the *draugr*. After it rises from the dead, it's said to have superhuman strength. It's sometimes a black or blue color and is supposed to smell really bad!

In Norse myths, draugr were usually mean or greedy people during their lives. After death, they sometimes guarded treasure in their graves.

Some say the undead creatures called draugr were Viking warriors during their life.

These countries of Northern Europe are called the Nordic countries. They are north and east of Ireland and the UK.

THE JIANGSHI

The next myth will take you to another **continent**: Asia. Chinese myths include a creature called *jiangshi*. These undead beings don't move well because their bodies became stiff after death. They hop from place to place! Sometimes they're called hopping vampires, though they don't feed on blood. Instead, they feed on people's life force.

Jiangshi are created several different ways in the myths, including improper burials and lightning strikes. (Jianghsi that transform quickly after death move faster than those who lie in their grave for longer.)

The idea of the jiangshi came from China but became popular across East Asia, especially in Japan and Taiwan, because of movies about them.

Behind the Myth

Jiangshi means "stiff **corpse**" in the Mandarin language.

In this photo, two men are dressed up as jiangshi.

NEXT STOP, HAITI

The most famous zombie tales come from Haiti. The word "zombie" does too! Haiti is one of the two countries on the island of Hispaniola in the Caribbean Sea. (The other is the Dominican Republic.) In the 1600s, Europeans **enslaved** West African peoples and brought them to Haiti to work.

Over time, some of these people mixed their African **religious** traditions with the Christian traditions of Europeans. This resulted in a religion called Vodou (or Voodoo). Undead *zombi* were part of Vodou beliefs.

THE BAHAMAS

Turks and Caicos Islands (U.K.)

HAITI

DOMINICAN REPUBLIC

British Virgin Islands (U.K.)

U.S. Virgin Islands

Navassa I. (U.S.)

JAMAICA

PUERTO RICO (U.S.)

This map of the Caribbean has a scale. This tool tells you distances in real life.

Behind the Myth

In the Kimbundu language, the word *nzúmbe* means "ghost." The Haitian French word *zombi* (which later became zombie) may come from this African language.

The enslaved people of Haiti were forced to work on farms and treated poorly.

In the Vodou tradition, someone uses magic to raise the dead and make this "zombi" do their bidding. Did this happen in L'Estère, Haiti?

Behind the Myth

Becoming a zombie through Vodou magic was a terrible fate. It meant being enslaved for all time.

L'Estère, Haiti, is south of the city of Gonaïves, in the country's northern **peninsula**. Find it on the map.

In 1980, a Haitian man named Clairvius Narcisse arrived on the doorstep of his sister, in the small community of L'Estère. She was shocked because he had died 20 years before! Clairvius said he had been given drugs that made him seem dead. After his burial, he was dug up by a Vodou priest and forced to work on a **sugarcane** farm. Some considered Clairvius a real-life zombie, though others didn't believe the story.

This artwork shows a zombie in a sugarcane field in Haiti.

ZOMBIES GO HOLLYWOOD

The Voudou stories of zombies and those of the myths of Europe and Asia may be a bit different from the zombie tales you know. In modern zombie stories, people become zombies a variety of ways.

Sometimes a disease, or illness, can "zombify" people in zombie tales. In still other stories, **radiation** creates zombies of the living or the dead. One of the most popular zombification methods is a bite or scratch from another zombie. A lot of these ideas came from movies.

People's real-life fears of radiation and dangerous chemicals **inspired** zombie stories.

The filmmaker George A. Romero was the first to put forward the idea of zombies as undead creatures who want to eat people. This was the plot of his 1968 movie *Night of the Living Dead*. The word "zombie" wasn't in that film, however. Romero used "ghouls."

Romero went on to make several more zombie movies that inspired other storytellers, including authors of books and creators of video games. A 1985 movie called *Return of the Night of the Living Dead* introduced the idea that zombies wanted to eat brains!

Behind the Myth

Some later zombie movies weren't scary at all. They were funny and poked fun at ideas about zombies.

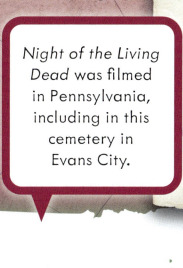

Night of the Living Dead was filmed in Pennsylvania, including in this cemetery in Evans City.

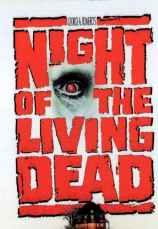

23

ZOMBIE REALITY?

Now that you've investigated some zombie myths around the world, do you believe in zombies? One scientist who studied the zombi Vodou tales of Haiti found out some Vodou followers made a mixture using a poison from the deadly pufferfish. This poison is known to cause **paralysis** (if not real death). Others doubt this could really zombify someone, though.

Zombie stories have been a way to explore certain ideas in a creative way. For example, zombie tales make people think about fears of death, enslavement, disease, and other issues.

Behind the Myth

In most stories, it's very hard to kill a zombie. Their brain has to be destroyed somehow.

One pufferfish contains enough poison to kill 30 people. There's a law in Haiti that makes it illegal to try to make others into zombies, using pufferfish poison or not.

ZOMBIE CULTURE

People today remain very interested in the idea of zombies. Have you ever seen a zombie walk? That's when a large group of people dress up like zombies and have a kind of parade. Thousands of people attend some of these events.

The largest zombie gathering was in Minneapolis, Minnesota, on October 11, 2014. More than 15,500 people showed up. And there doesn't seem to be any signs of zombie TV shows, movies, and video games going away soon. This creature just won't die!

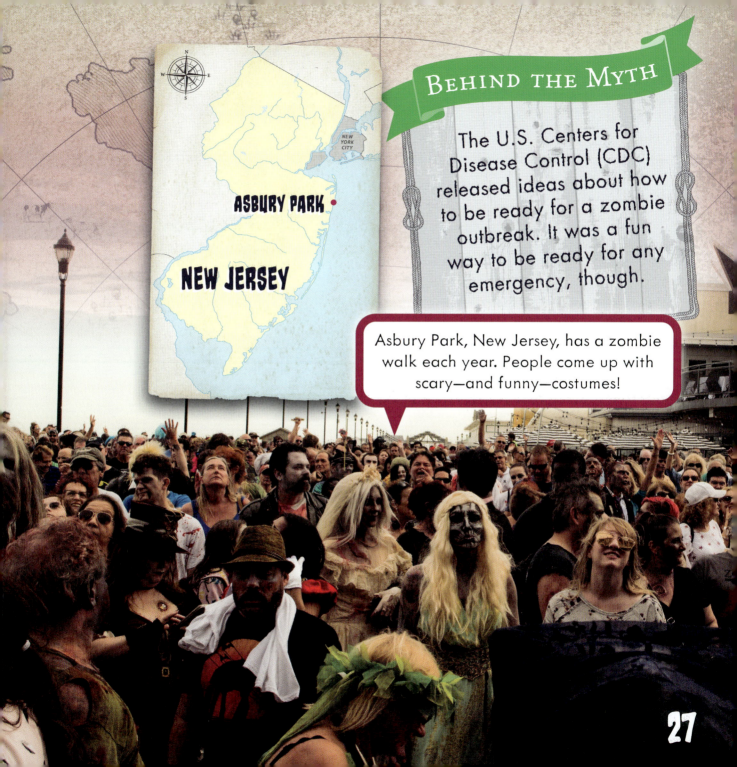

ASBURY PARK

NEW JERSEY

BEHIND THE MYTH

The U.S. Centers for Disease Control (CDC) released ideas about how to be ready for a zombie outbreak. It was a fun way to be ready for any emergency, though.

Asbury Park, New Jersey, has a zombie walk each year. People come up with scary—and funny—costumes!

ZOMBIES ON THE MAP

Minneapolis, Minnesota—The largest gathering of people dressed as zombies happened here.

Ireland and England—Graves display evidence that may show a belief that the dead could rise.

Pennsylvania—George A. Romero's *Night of the Living Dead* was filmed here, inspiring modern zombie tales.

Haiti—The *zombi* is an idea from the Vodou religion.

GLOSSARY

archaeologist: A scientist who studies past human life and activities.

continent: One of Earth's seven great landmasses.

corpse: A dead body.

decaying: Becoming more damaged.

enslaved: Having to do with being owned by another person and forced to work without pay under terrible conditions.

inspire: To cause someone to want to do something.

myth: A story that was told by a people to explain a practice, belief, or natural event.

paralysis: The state of being unable to move.

peninsula: A narrow piece of land that extends into water from the mainland.

radiation: Waves of energy.

religious: Having to do with religion, or a belief in and way of honoring a god or gods.

revenge: Harm done to punish someone for harm that they have done to someone else.

sugarcane: A plant from whose tall thick stems sugar can be produced.

For More Information

Books

Erickson, Marty. *Zombies*. Mankato, MN: Child's World, 2022.

Hamilton, Sue L. *The World's Scariest Zombies*. Minneapolis, MN: A&D Xtreme, 2022.

Moon, Walt K. *Zombies*. San Diego, CA: BrightPoint Press, 2022.

Websites

Curious Kids: Are Zombies Real?
theconversation.com/curious-kids-are-zombies-real-79347#
Read more about the zombies of Haitian lore.

Zombie
kids.britannica.com/kids/article/zombie/600661
Read more about this scary undead creature.

Publisher's note to educators and parents: Our editors have carefully reviewed these websites to ensure that they are suitable for students. Many websites change frequently, however, and we cannot guarantee that a site's future contents will continue to meet our high standards of quality and educational value. Be advised that students should be closely supervised whenever they access the internet.

INDEX

Asia, 14, 15, 20

Caribbean, 16, 17

China, 14, 15, 29

biting, 10, 20

brains, 4, 22, 25

England, 8, 10, 11, 29

enslavement, 16, 17, 18, 24

graves, 6, 8, 10, 12, 14, 28

Greece, 6, 7, 8

Haiti, 16, 17, 18, 19, 20, 24, 25, 28

Ireland, 10, 11, 12, 13, 28

Minnesota, 26, 28

movies, 15, 20, 22, 26

Narcisse, Clairvius, 19

New Jersey, 27

Nordic countries, 12, 13, 29

Pennsylvania, 23, 28

pufferfish, 24, 25

radiation, 20, 21

Romero, George A., 22, 28

TV shows, 26

United Kingdom, 11, 12, 13

video games, 22, 26

Vodou, 16, 18, 19, 20, 24, 28

zombie walks, 26, 27